SHE'S ABOUT BUSINESS

SHE'S ABOUT BUSINESS
Single, Saved,
and Healed

DIATHE GARNES

ISBN: Softcover   978-1-7960-1909-4
             eBook   978-1-7960-1917-9

Print information available on the last page.

Rev. date: 03/04/2019

To order additional copies of this book, contact:
Xlibris
1-888-795-4274
www.Xlibris.com
Orders@Xlibris.com
792421

Contents

Preface

It's been over ten years since I first sought the Lord in regard to preparation for marriage and singleness. I have to admit that I wasn't really interested in being married per se'. I was more interested in His will for my life and because those around me kept telling me that it was His will for me to be married, I decided to go directly to the source for answers. I have to admit I hadn't been too blessed in love up until that point, which is probably why I wasn't in a hurry to get married. But there was something about marriage, as it was meant to be according to the Word of God that intrigued me.

Even though it's been so long ago, I remember it like it was yesterday. I don't know if I picked a random scripture from the Bible or if I found it in my reading, but days after I began to seek the Lord about marriage, Isaiah 54:5 was posted all over the mirrors, walls, and even the refrigerator of my home.

For thy Maker is thine husband; the Lord of hosts is his name; and thy Redeemer the
Holy One of Israel; The God of the whole earth shall he be called. – Isaiah 54:5 KJV

What I learned from that experience was that even when single in the natural, I was married in the spirit to my Maker! Instead of longing for a husband, my goal needed to shift towards seeking a deeper relationship with my Maker; one that would mimic the marriage in the natural to my earthly husband...one that would prepare me for being a wife. During your season of singleness, whether it is short or long, remember that you are never alone. If you allow the process to take its course and endure it openly and not grudgingly, then you will allow yourself to be prepared and equipped by the Most-High God!

This little book was designed to show you how! It's packed with information that I gained during my times of prayer and study and it's my prayer that even though it's small, it will give you a big return during your season as a single woman and even a bigger one during your marriage!

Introduction

The goal of this book is to help readers live meaningfully during their season of singleness or while preparing for a Godly union, avoiding despair and discouragement. The book was built on the principle of utilizing God's Word to help better understand the desires of one's heart so that those desires are better aligned with the desires of God's heart.

This book is designed for women seeking to benefit from scriptural teachings during their season of singleness or who are preparing for a Godly union with a man and want to:

- Understand how to prepare for marriage.
- Recognize and identify possible generational curses.
- Differentiate between shame, condemnation, conviction, and Godly guilt.
- Identify ungodly soul ties and how to destroy them.
- Identify prayers for sustenance.
- Learn to pray more strategic and meaningful prayers for the relationships in her life.

This book wasn't written in the traditional, summary format, but instead I use bullets and sections to help you remember important points, find important points quickly, and read through the book quickly or multiple times if needed.

My thought process with this book was the same as the other books in the She's About Business Series, and that is to avoid filling the pages with filler information and simply get down to the important points!

I also included a journal section for you to write out the prayers of your heart for your relationship with God, with yourself, and with your future or current mate. You can also use the journal section to express any ideas or thoughts that you have as you're reading the book.

I pray that this book blesses your life, and your future or current marriage!

Godly Marriage

PREPARING FOR MARRIAGE

The journey that got me to the point of doing this book began years ago with the Lord leading me to post Isaiah 54:5 all around my home so that I'd be reminded of how He was preparing me. The scripture reads…

4 "Do not fear, for you will not be ashamed;
   Neither be disgraced, for you will not be put to shame;
   For you will forget the shame of your youth,
   And will not remember the reproach of your widowhood anymore.
   Isaiah 54: 4 (NKJV)

5 For your Maker is your husband,
   The Lord of hosts is His name;
   And your Redeemer is the Holy One of Israel; He is called the God of the whole earth.
   Isaiah 54: 5 (NKJV)

Here are some key points learned from my personal journey and study:

- **In the absence of a husband, a woman who is a Child of God, is already a wife!**

- **That's right...if you are single in the natural and saved in the spirit, you are married to the Most-High God! Now, let that sink in for a minute! Our marriage to God in the spirit, prepares us for our marriage to our human husband in the natural. So, to you who are getting discouraged because you are single in the natural, you may be missing your opportunity to walk in your marriage to the Most-High God, and in fact missing your opportunity to allow Him to prepare you for marriage in the natural.**

You may be wondering how you can take full advantage of your season of singleness to allow the Lord to develop your character in preparation for marriage.

You can do this by beginning to act like you are married to Jesus! This is not meant to be some weird thing where you are in some weird relationship with Jesus...the kind that makes people give you the side eye. It's really about you beginning to see yourself as a wife. This will help prepare you for your natural marriage.

- **Shop like someone who was married in the natural.** Make sure that your home is stocked with the proper household toiletries and supplies. I'm sure there are few things more annoying than a hardworking man coming home after a long day and discovering that there is no toilet paper when he needs it.
- **Dress up like someone who wants to look nice for your husband.** You don't have to always look your best when your married, because just like God, your husband will see you and should love you even at your worst. But we should never take for granted the loving acceptance that comes with the marriage relationship. Always put forth your best effort to look your best as a sign of love for yourself and your mate.
- **Keep a comfortable home.** Not everyone is a neat freak able to keep a home clean enough to eat off the floors. But, do your best to keep your hoe comfortable for your family and guests. Wash the dishes, make your bed, and vacuum regularly. Don't do these things as a means of impressing an earthly man but do them as a symbol of commitment because these are the things that we may let slide when there is no one to see them.

- **Provide for your household well.** This is the overall distinction of a virtuous woman. She is about the business of taking care of her home and her family. This means making sure that there is adequate food in the home, even if you are not equipped with the skill or desire to be the primary cook of the home. This means doing your best to ensure that bills are cared for adequately. Operate your home with wisdom and care.
- **Change your mindset.** Understand that it is God's desire to give you the desires He has put on your heart according to Psalms 37:4 which says, "Delight yourself in the LORD, And He will give you the desires and petitions of your heart." Psalm 37:4 AMP

  ❖ If you are one who delights yourself in the Lord and a Godly marriage is a desire and petition of your heart, chances are, God gave you that desire, and it is also His Will ---- If it is His Will, then it means that you were born to do it! ---- But, even when are born to do something, training is still required and that is why the preparation is necessary.

FOOD FOR THOUGHT

- Some will ask if all this is true, then why is it that some folks marry so young not having gone through a preparation period.
- First, I would say to them that not all those who marry are called to do so at that time or they may not be called to marry those who they end up marrying.
- Depending on the particular purpose and call on your life in other areas, God may give you the grace to get married early and teach you as you go, how to sustain a long, healthy, happy marriage.
- Likewise, He may require the extension of your singleness in order to build you up in the areas needed to fulfill your purpose.
- Every person is different. Which brings me to the second thing that God showed me.

Celibacy – The Calling

THE DESIRE TO MARRY

Because many of us have been told that not everyone is meant to be married, many who have the desire to marry, give up hope, because they believe that have been called to be single… even though they truly desire marriage.

Psalms 37:4 "Delight yourself in the LORD, And He will give you the desires and petitions of your heart." Psalm 37:4 AMP

This takes us back to Psalms 37:4. This scripture teaches us that when we delight ourselves in the Lord, he has promised to give us the desires of our hearts.

When God is promising to give us the desires of our hearts, would He do so for ungodly desires?

- God would only promise to give us the desires of our hearts with the expectations that those desires are Godly.
- God would not grant you a desire that is ungodly because that would lead you to sin, whereas a Godly desire would end up glorifying Him.

- A Godly marriage creates a Godly covenant and if one has a desire for such a marriage, then we can trust that God would be pleased with such a desire, and therefore grant it.

THE GIFT OF CELIBACY

Matthew 19:9-12 NIV (Read below)

Jesus says, "I tell you that anyone who divorces his wife, except for marital unfaithfulness, and marries another woman commits adultery.' The disciples said to him, 'If this is the situation between a husband and wife, it is better not to marry.' Jesus replied, 'Not everyone can accept this word, but only those to whom it has been given. For some are eunuchs because they were born that way; others were made that way by men; and others have renounced marriage because of the kingdom of heaven. The one who can accept this should accept it."

- ○ **The phrase "only those to whom it has been given" refers to people receiving what some call "the gift of celibacy" or "the gift of singleness."** Regardless of what we call the gift, Jesus teaches that most people do not naturally desire to remain single and celibate for a lifetime.
- ○ **The exceptions are those who have "renounced marriage" for the kingdom's sake or because of the acts of man** (i.e. abuse or mistreatment). Such celibates have received a special gift from God.

1 Corinthians 7 NIV (Various scriptures from chapter read below)

- In this chapter Paul states that it is not wrong to get married, but that it is better if a Christian can stay single. (The reason is that a married man's attention is "divided" between pleasing the Lord and pleasing his wife; a single man is free to be more focused on the Lord's work, verses 32-34.)
- Paul says, "I wish that all men were [unmarried] as I am. But each man has his own gift from God; one has this gift, another has that" (verse 7).
- Paul is careful to state that this is "a view, not . . . a command" (verse 6). The ability to stay single and serve God apart from marriage is a gift. Paul and some others had the gift but not everyone does.

- As we see, the Bible does not explicitly call this "the gift of celibacy," but it does express that the ability to remain unmarried to serve God more fully is a gift. Most adults desire marriage, and this desire is not sinful. For the true child of God, having a desire for Godly marriage is natural and an indication that marriage is indeed your portion.

Season of Singleness

<u>DOES THE DEVIL WANT TO KEEP ME SINGLE?</u>

I hear this question a lot and I have had this thought many times myself.

I've gone to God about it and inquired of Him very righteously and fervently, asking why He would allow the enemy to do such a thing. The answer always came back to me in the form of His Word.

Isaiah 54:17, Romans 8:28

- What this tells me is that if God says yes to my marriage, then no devil in hell can say no to it…unless of course I allow it.
- I believe that the answer to the above question is, yes, Satan does want to keep all of God's children from Godly marriages.

2 Corinthians 4:4, Ephesians 5

1. **Satan's main goal is to keep people from receiving Jesus Christ. 2 Corinthians 4:4 tells us that the enemy blinds the mind of the unsaved so that they will not be able to see the light of the message of the gospel. But, once he has failed at this and you do receive Jesus, then his next goal is to keep you from giving God glory. Satan hates anything that will give God glory.**

- In Ephesians 5 we learn that God wants His glory to shine through the union of marriage. The love, self-sacrifice, knowledge and understanding of one another and mutual submission are aspects of marriage that reflect the glory of everything that Jesus is. If you are unwillingly single or in an unhappy marriage, that is one less way you can glorify God.

TOOLS THE ENEMY USES TO KEEP YOU SINGLE

The manipulation of Pride and selfishness

John 8:44

2. **Satan will destroy love relationships by allowing you to take your focus off God or your significant other and focus only on self.**

- If you find yourself going through the same types of situations repeatedly in relationships, it could be a sign that the enemy is causing you to focus on self.
- Having continuous negative thoughts about your relationship such as, "this is too hard, this is unfair, I don't have to settle for this, I have to settle for this because I can't do better, I've done all I can, I'll never get married, etc.… could all indicate that you're being deceived. In John 8:44, Jesus speaks of the enemy saying, "there is no truth in him. When he lies, he speaks his native language, for he is a liar and the father of lies."
- Take note of the negative thoughts that were persistent during your last or current relationship and ask yourself if they were true.
- Also ask yourself if they negatively affected the relationship?

  o If they were lies and they negatively affected your relationship, chances are you were being deceived and manipulated by the enemy.

Generational Curses

Genesis 4:9-11, Genesis 9:20-25, Deuteronomy 7:25-26, Joshua 6:26, 2 Kings 9:30-34, Psalms 119:21

3. **The enemy can block progress in your life, even in marriage because of generational curses. Look at your family history for signs of generational curses.**

- If the people in your family often fail to get married, suffer many divorces, or go from failed relationship to failed relationship, there may be a generational curse in existence.

Generational curses can come as the result of the recent or distant past sin of family members. Generational curses usually stem from one of these things:

- The shedding of innocent blood. (Like Cain in Genesis 4:911)
- Sexual perversion. (Like Canaan the grandson of Noah who saw him naked and made a mockery of him in **Genesis 9:20-25)**
- Bringing abominations, morally disgusting objects, or idols into your house. (As described in Deuteronomy 7:25-26)
- Rebuilding what God destroyed. When God has delivered someone from something, cursed is the one who reintroduces it into their lives.
  (As described in Joshua 6:26)
- Operating in the spirit of Jezebel with signs such as being controlling, manipulative, power hungry, and seducing.
  (As described in (2 Kings 9:30-34)
- Being arrogant and proud. (As described in Psalms 119:21)

The truth is, many of our ancestors did things to bring curses upon us.

- Especially in our native lands, innocent blood was shed, there was sexual perversion, idols were worshipped, etc.…
- Today, we ourselves may do things to bring curses upon ourselves and future generations, such as being bad influences on others (rebuilding what God has torn down) operating in the Jezebel spirit and being arrogant and proud.
- Thankfully, because of God's great mercy, generational curses can be broken through repentance, denouncing them, and the application of the Blood of Jesus.

Shame and Condemnation

1 John 1:9, Romans 8:1

4. **The enemy can cause feelings of shame and condemnation that lead you to act a certain way within relationships.** Shame and condemnation are the opposite of conviction and Godly guilt.

How to Know the Difference:

- **Condemnation (leads you to be ashamed or feel hated by God)**
- **Conviction (leads you to repentance)**
- **Shame (Makes you feel embarrassed or unworthy)**
- **Godly Guilt (Causes you to feel bad when you sin)**

- If you feel shame and condemnation for past mistakes, you may constantly date people who you are unequally yoked with.
- You may continue to go through cycles of dating people who are not good for you because you think that's all that you deserve.
- Or, because of shame and condemnation that comes in the form of a fear of failing again or of getting hurt, you may simply avoid dating all together.

  - The enemy tells you that you are incapable of being successful in a relationship, so you decide there is no need to try again.

- The enemy especially loves to use past sexual sin to cause you to feel shame and condemnation.

  - He tells you that you're used up. Or, that you should not have done this or that.

  - Or, that no one will ever want you if they found out what you've done.

- Remember that he can only lie and there is no truth in him.

  - Reject his lies and believe what God said in 1 John 1:9.

o   If we confess our sins, God is faithful and just to forgive us and purify us from all unrighteousness. There is no condemnation (needed) for those who are in Christ Jesus (Romans 8:1).

Matthew 10:28 - Do not be afraid of those who kill the body but cannot kill the soul. Rather, be afraid of the One who can destroy both soul and body in hell.

Fear

5.   **The enemy can use fear to keep you single.**

- If you have an unhealthy, unnatural fear of being hurt in a relationship, this could be a sign that the enemy is again deceiving you.
- Fear is never of God unless it is a healthy, reverent fear of God.

    o   The book of Matthew teaches us to fear only God, who can destroy both soul and body in hell" (Matthew 10:28).

- You should protect your heart, but you do so by giving your heart first to God, not by hiding it away and throwing away the key.
- This isn't to say that we should just date without consideration for protecting our hearts.

    o   But, when we are so afraid to try to give our hearts again, it's almost like saying that we cannot continue in life if the relationship doesn't work out.

- You should never elevate a relationship so high that you feel like you cannot live without it.
- That type of validation should only be given to God.

    o   Only Christ deserves that place in your heart.

- Trust Him to protect you, give you wisdom and discernment to make the proper choses within a relationship.
- If you keep this proper order, God will protect you from being broken by any relationship, therefore you have no reason to fear.

Unknowingly making an idol out of a love relationship/marriage

Romans 12:2 NIV Do not conform to the pattern of this world but be transformed by the renewing of your mind. Then you will be able to test and approve what God's will is—his good, pleasing and perfect will.

6. **The enemy can cause you to be overzealous in your desire for a relationship.**

- This means that you believe that a love relationship or marriage is the only thing that will ever make you happy.
- You want a marriage so bad that it becomes an idol to you.

    o You'll do anything to get your idol, even at the detriment to your spiritual, mental, or physical well-being.

    o The loving God that we serve would never bless one of His children with an idol because He knows that this idol would replace Him in your heart.

    o He knows that this will lead to hardship and heartache and loves you too much to allow it.

- The bottom line is that we should never give the enemy too much credit for what he can and can't do in our lives.

    o The only way that any trick or trap of the enemy will work against us is if we allow it.

    o How do we allow him this power over our lives? By taking no action against it.

    o Our best weapon against the enemy is prayer and repentance.

Spiritual Roadblocks

(THINGS THAT KEEP US FROM OVERCOMING THE ENENMY IN THIS AREA)

WORKING THROUGH FRUSTRATIONS

Romans 8:28, 2 Corinthians 12:7-10 (Integrated below)

I've learned the hard way that God doesn't guarantee the joys of the world for his children…physical health, wealth, success, children or marriage are not promised to us.

- God is very committed to giving us the very finest in life and that can honestly mean different things for different people. But, His love for us means that He will only give it to us, when and if it's best for us.
- There is no exception to this rule for it is truly God's Will that all things work out for our good (Romans 8:28).

This means that no matter how bad we want it or how right WE believe that it is for us, God will not change His mind about what's best. In this case, Father really does know best!

- Sure, it may hurt us or make us feel persecuted, abandoned or weakened due to the aching we feel for the thing that we long for, but often in our weakness we are made strong like the apostle Paul in (2 Corinthians 12:710).
- Paul recognizes that the thorn in his side, though uncomfortable, made him stronger in his weakness and kept him from becoming boastful or conceited.
- Believe it or not, if God gave us everything that we wanted, when we wanted it, we would not be humble, modest Christians about it.

Many run away from God out of Frustration

Even though God only wants to give us the best, and even though not getting what we want when we want is usually best for us, we are still often tempted to abandon God, giving up on His plan for us and even turn our backs on Him out of sheer frustration.

- It's laughable, but we truly do believe that we know what's best for ourselves and go as far as trying to convince God to change His mind because of our bickering and whining.
- Thankfully for us God does not change His mind about what's best for us.
- His knowledge is infinite and ours is so minute when compared.
- Instead of running away from God, we truly should be running to Him and praying to Him consistently during our time of singleness.

We should remain committed to staying in God's Will even when we're frustrated?

- When you're frustrated, hurt, and still wanting what you want, still refuse to turn away from God. Here's how can begin to pray daily, surrendering your desires to Him.

Prayers to Help You Sustain and Maintain During Singleness

10 PRAYERS

Here are 10 prayers to help you through your time of singleness while also growing your faith and your relationship with your Father.

1. **I repent from all past and present sins of my ancestors and myself.**

   "But if they confess their iniquity and THE INIQUITY OF THEIR FATHERS, with their unfaithfulness in which they were unfaithful to Me, and that they also have walked contrary to Me … then I will remember My covenant with Jacob, and My covenant with Isaac and My covenant with Abraham I will remember …" Leviticus 26:40, 42 NKJV

PRAYER:
   Lord, I know not all the sins of my ancestors, but if there have been any curses placed on my life or the life of my future generations because

of The shedding of innocent blood, Sexual perversion, the bringing in the home or worship of abominations, morally disgusting objects, or idols, the rebuilding of what God destroyed, the operating in the spirit of Jezebel with signs such as being controlling, manipulative, power hungry, and seducing, or being arrogant and proud, rejecting your power, glory and authority, I repent right now in the name of Jesus. I repent of any of these sins that I have done. I repent of and break all covenants with the enemy that have allowed my life to be cursed in any way and I ask for forgiveness. I plead the blood of Jesus over every area where a curse has operated up until this time in my life. I plead the blood of Jesus over the lives of my children and all future generations.

2. **Fulfill my heart's greatest desires.**

"And I tell you, ask, and it will be given to you; seek, and you will find; knock, and it will be opened to you." Luke 11:9 ESV

Of all the things that could be your greatest dream, the one thing that will bring you the most peace, success and love is to pray: Jesus, please be my greatest dream. I want to love You more.

Then, your prayer for your greatest dream to be fulfilled will be one that you can ensure will not only give God glory, but give you peace during your successes, failures, gains, and losses…whether married or unmarried.

3. **Not my will, but yours, be done.**

"Father, if you are willing, remove this cup from me. Nevertheless, not my will, but yours, be done." Luke 22:42 ESV

PRAYER:
Lord oh God, the words that comforted Jesus while bearing the burden of the cross can most certainly comfort me during my time of singleness." Help me to make the most of my time of singleness and to prepare for marriage if that is your will for my life. Help me to see all that you have planned for me. Anchor my heart in you and not in marriage.

4. **Help me to know you and your ways as deeply as possible while I am single.**

"You will seek Me and find Me when you seek Me with all your heart." Jeremiah 29:13 NIV

"Call to Me and I will answer you and tell you great and wondrous things you do not know." Jeremiah 33:3 NIV

PRAYER:

Lord show me more of you while I can give you my full attention. Help me to structure my life so that it gives you glory whether I'm married or single. Help me to remember Lord that you are the prize in my life, not marriage or any other person, thing, or condition.

5. **Allow my joy and fullness of life while single to shine a light upon Your goodness.**

"And the peace of God, which surpasses all understanding, will guard your hearts and your minds in Christ Jesus." Philippians 4:7 ESV

PRAYER:

Lord let not my condition of singleness or married hinder the use of my gifts, talents, and abilities to grow Your Kingdom. Let peace be my garment while I am single and when I am married. Let others see your goodness when they see the joy which is present in my life, regardless of my relationship status.

6. **Help me to not seek for happiness from any other person. Help me to be satisfied by you.**

"These things I have spoken to you, that my joy may be in you, and that your joy may be full." John 16:33 ESV

PRAYER:

Help me to understand that no spouse, no friend, no accomplishment or goal is worthy of filling the space in my heart that is meant for you. When my heart wants to wander as it often does, help it to remember that you are more than enough. Help me to remember oh Lord, that the pecking order of the loves in my life always begins with you.

7. **Give me faith to forgive those who have hurt me and not become bitter. Give me faith to trust you even when I feel alone and disappointed.**

"Get rid of all bitterness, rage and anger, brawling and slander, along with every form of malice." Ephesians 4:31 NIV

"And we know that all things work together for good to them that love God, to them who are the called according to his purpose." Romans 8:28 KJV

PRAYER:

Lord, help me to forgive those who have hurt me, abandoned me, rejected, or abused me. Help my heart not become bitter and hindered in my ability to love freely again. Lord sometimes I get lonely. During those times, my faith in you is tested and I often feel disappointment. Help me Lord to know that I am never alone for you are with me always. Help me to remember that all things, even my singleness are working for my good.

8. **Send me the right support system to love me and not judge me.**

"And I will give you shepherds after my own heart, who will feed you with knowledge and understanding." Jeremiah 3:15 ESV

"Do not be misled: "Bad company corrupts good character.""

1 Corinthians 15:33 NIV

PRAYER:

Father bring people around me who genuinely love me, but most importantly, who genuinely love you. Allow them to see the glory in the peace that I have during my time of singleness and as I wait on you to revel my mate. Allow them to avoid judgment of my condition of singleness, and instead help me to mature and grow in preparation for the ministry you have for me. Help me to see myself through their eyes and learn from their faith, maturity, words of encouragement and strength. Make me a stronger, more relevant member of the body of Christ serving your people the way you have called me to. Help me avoid hiding myself away in isolation and feeling sorry for myself. Help me to refrain from having a "what about me attitude" as I watch others marry, which is self-centeredness. Help me to learn from those you place in my life and enjoy the friendships established during this time.

9. **Help me to avoid conforming to the world's standards on dating. Help me to date in a way that glorifies you and makes you proud.**

"It is my prayer that your love may abound more and more, with knowledge and all discernment, so that you may approve what is excellent, and so be pure and blameless for the day of Christ, filled with the fruit of righteousness that comes through Jesus Christ, to the glory and praise of God." Philippians 1:9-11 ESV

"Do not be unequally yoked together with unbelievers. For what fellowship has righteousness with lawlessness? And what communion has light with darkness? And what accord has Christ with Belial? Or what part has a believer with an unbeliever? And what agreement has the temple of God with idols? For you are the temple of the living God." (2 Corinthians 6:14-16) NKJV

PRAYER:

Lord, help me not to date the way that the world dates, moving too fast and mixing with people simply based on how they look or how they make me feel. Help me to remember who I am and who I represent when I'm dating. Help me to use discernment when choosing who to date. Give me clarity so that I can see the true nature of any relationship I consider establishing. Guard me from impurity in thought and deed. Help me to exhibit the traits of Christ during every date, conversation, and interaction while dating. Help me to demonstrate your hand on my life so that all will know that I am yours before anyone's.

10. **Give me a heart to forgive past offenses against me and keep my heart from bitterness.**

"When he was reviled, he did not revile in return; when he suffered, he did not threaten, but continued entrusting himself to him who judges justly." 1 Peter 2:23 ESV

"See to it that no one fails to obtain the grace of God; that no "root of bitterness" springs up and causes trouble, and by it many become defiled;" Hebrews 12:15 ESV

PRAYER:

Lord, if Jesus was so greatly injured by the acts of others yet did not retaliate or allow bitterness to be His portion, help me to do the same for those who have injured me knowingly or unknowingly. Help me to entrust myself to You, the one who judges justly. Help me to move forward in life with no roots of bitterness lingering in my heart, causing trouble in my relationships and defiling my life. Help me to live a life without offense and help me to end all negative soul ties which I am still connected to due to unforgiveness.

Soul Ties

THE DANGERS OF SOUL TIES

The theory of soul ties is one that is not based in religion but on the science of people and how we are build. But scripture does clearly depict the power and realness of soul ties.

1 Samuel 18:1, 1 Corinthians 6:16

"As soon as he had finished speaking to Saul, the soul of Jonathan was knit to the soul of David, and Jonathan loved him as his own soul." 1 Samuel 18:1 ESV

"Or do you not know that he who is joined to a prostitute becomes one body with her? For, as it is written, "The two will become one flesh." 1 Corinthians 6:16 ESV

Key Points About Soul Ties

- We are spiritual beings, so we connect not only physically but spiritually as well.
- The strongest soul ties come from sex, but they can also be created with family members, platonic friends, coworkers, and even people you've never met through unhealthy fixations and obsessions.
- Emotionally rich, healthy, and Godly soul ties are easier to identify than negative soul ties.

- Negative soul ties often enhance already existing strongholds in your life.
- Negative soul ties can wear not only on you, but on your support base as well.
- Negative soul ties are often equally damaging, but more often, one person is benefitting more and taking advantage of the situation more than the other. This can feel like a very abusive situation to the person who is being taken advantage of.

EXPLANATION OF SEXUAL SOUL TIES

There's a reason God wants sex to be between a husband and a wife. Intercourse intertwines your energy with that of the other person. It is a very intimate act, both in the natural and in the Spirit.

Soul tie Explanation: Imagine two pieces of thick cardboard being glued together using crazy glue and then pulled apart violently. Each piece will show the signs of being put together and pulled apart. One side will have remnants of itself torn away, while the other will now carry the remnants of the other. Likewise, with sex, a man has parts of himself given away to the woman, and the woman takes on and carries the remnants of the man. The trouble with having multiple sexual partners is that men give fragments of themselves away to many women, and women carry around fragments of multiple men. This creates emotional dysfunction and relational issues.

IDENTIFYING NEGATIVE SOUL TIES

1. You feel a sense of wrongness after sex. Sex is intended to be physically and emotionally gratifying. If you feel used, dirty, unsure, or convicted after sex, stop!

2. You feel a sense of being torn between your head and your heart in the relationship. You go back and forth about whether or not you should leave or stay.

3. You feel a sense of being tormented or abused, even if not physically or verbally. No matter how hard you try, the relationship never feels right and no matter how hard you try to fix it, it doesn't work. You are often blamed for the situation or told you need to change or improve.

4. The other person either constantly passes blame to you or takes all the blame on themselves in a "it's not you, it's me" type of way. When taking the blame, they make no or little effort to change. When passing the blame to you, their claims are based on unfounded accusations and they can offer no feedback for how to improve things.

5. Your support base is fed up! Those who truly love you are finding it hard to exist in the mess of your negative relationship. Many of them who have been tried and true are tucking tail and leaving you and your mess behind. Don't blame them! It really is hard to watch someone you love being involved in a negative soul tie relationship.

HOW TO BREAK A SOUL TIE

1. Make a decision and truly mean it. Be resolved to break the soul tie, acknowledging that it is harmful to your well-being.

2. Pray and ask for help in untangling the mess of a knot you've allowed yourself to be tangled in. Ask for forgiveness for any sin, repent and then believe that you are forgiven.

3. Renounce the soul tie. Verbally renounce the connection and verbally say, "I break my soul tie with _____."

4. Be willing to forgive the person, even if they don't want to be forgiven. Being willing to forgive and let go of any offenses is a huge determining factor in whether you'll be able to successfully break a negative soul tie.

5. In theory, it's like using the ultimate act of love to quench the negative leftovers of the relationship.

Forgiveness

WHY WE MUST FORGIVE

We've all heard them before. "Forgive and forget," "let bygones be bygones," etc....

- These forgiveness clichés are in line with spiritual teaching on forgiveness, but they do little to encourage us to forgive the most damaging offenses we can suffer...those of the heart.
- Not only is forgiveness a principle taught by Jesus as a determining factor on our receiving forgiveness from God, but it's also vital for us moving on into happy marriages without baggage.
- What you can't forgive, you cannot release.
- Unforgiveness and bitterness towards someone keeps you tied to them.
- I believe that some people actually use unforgiveness as a tie that binds them to another; a last-ditch effort to stay connected by any means necessary.
- But staying connected in this way also means not moving on.

WHY IS FORGIVENESS HARD?

- With all that the bible teaches us about forgiveness, why is forgiveness still so hard?
- In my study of forgiveness, I found that many people don't really understand the way that forgiveness works and simply try to force their way through the process head on with an attitude of "I'm going to do this simply because I must."
- They say, "I forgive you/them/him/her... but their heart, actions and attitude say something totally different.
- They do it more out of obligation to do it than from a true understanding of the process and a true desire to be free of the offense.
- Why are they/we getting it so wrong?

Let's look at Luke 17:3.

It reads, "So watch yourselves. "If your brother or sister sins against you, rebuke them; and if they repent, forgive them." (Luke 17:3) NIV

- According to this scripture if a brother or sister (another saved individual) sins against you, you have a duty to rebuke (acknowledge their wrong doing in a Godly way) and IF they repent (ask for forgiveness and change their mind, attitude, or behavior) ...
- THEN we are to forgive them.
- When dealing with another child of God, forgiveness concerns the restoration of a relationship.
- But there are stipulations that we often ignore because we simply pretend to forgive to keep the relationship going or forgive those who have not asked to be forgiven.
- When we pretend to forgive, we hold on to offenses and bitterness grows, making it impossible to completely restore a relationship.
- When we forgive those, who have not asked for forgiveness, (if they repent) we try to carry on a relationship with someone who may very well continue to exhibit the same negative behaviors and attitudes.
- Either scenario leads us down a road of repeated negative experiences within relationships.
- True forgiveness comes from a heart that understands the process of forgiveness.

- This means rebuking the offense in a Godly manner, and honestly observing whether the other person has a repentant heart or not.
- If they do not, this may mean that the relationship cannot be restored and moving on is best.
- In cases such as these, we must be willing to let go of the relationship and accept that its season in our lives is over.
- We must be willing to let go of offenses and bitterness and have a heart that is ready and willing to forgive when there is repentance.

KEY POINTS ABOUT FORGIVENESS

This is just the same way that God deals with us.

- We mistakenly think that God is sitting in Heaven just automatically forgiving all our sins as soon as we do them.
- On the contrary, He waits with a kind, loving, and gentle heart for the time when we repent of those sins, then He is gracious enough to forgive.
- We should model this behavior and forgive when those who have sinned against us are willing to listen to our reproof of their behavior and repent.

Understanding forgiveness in this way means:

- Being *willing* to forgive those who have not yet repented for past hurts. When and if they repent (apologize, ask for forgiveness), you must have a heart that is willing to receive their request and accept it.
- Offering forgiveness to those who have repented for their offenses against us and being willing to move on.

These gestures show maturity and will ensure that we are ready to walk into a marriage that will be able to glorify God.

- Marriage is not easy, and there will be many opportunities to offer and be forgiven.

- If you walk into a new relationship towing unforgiveness of past offenses along with you, chances are, you'll repeat that same behavior in the new relationship.
- If you are able to acknowledge and understand any reasons why you have difficulty forgiving it will move, you one step closer to becoming the woman you are meant to be. Self-knowledge and awareness are key!

Personality Test

One of the best ways to prepare for a serious, committed relationship and potentially marriage is to first get to know God on a closer level, which has been what this book aims to do.

- Another important piece of the puzzle is getting to know yourself on a deeper and closer level, which is also a goal of this book.
- That way, when in a relationship you won't need the other person to define who you are.
- You should be fully aware of who you are in Christ, but also of the distinct characteristics and traits that make you who you are.

That is why I want to recommend that you take a free personality test to help you determine your personality type.

Also, as a follow up to reading this book, I'm also suggesting that you find a life coach, therapist, or counselor who can work with you one-on-one to discuss with you:

- Your test results and how these affect your relationships.
- Anything else you may want to discuss from the book.

Ge started by simply typing the link below into your web browser to take your personality test when you're ready. If for any reason or at any time this link is not available, please search for another personality test that you have researched and feel can help you get the best understanding of your personality.

I selected the 16 Personality test to recommend here because it was the one that I felt was the most accurate in its description of my personality and gave me the most understanding on how my personality affects my relationships. It also gave me a better understanding of myself and how and why I operate the way that I do in relationships.

It was truly eye opening and I believe it will be for you too!

- **https://www.16personalities.com/freehttps://www.16personalities.com/free-personality-test personality-test**

Your Heart: Desires Fulfilled and Healed

"May he give you the desire of your heart
and make all your plans succeed."
Psalm 20:4 NIV

WHAT DO YOU DESIRE?

One of the greatest parts about truly getting to know yourself is becoming comfortable with the things you truly want… your heart's desires. For some reason, people are encouraged to pray for everything they want, from material things, to healing, to world peace…but are discouraged from praying for a God ordained mate. This is mind blowing to me.

I've heard a lot of the negativity from those who feel that praying for a spouse is wrong and I disagree with it wholeheartedly. I encourage you to pray for your spouse just as you would any other thing that is concerning you. Not only should we pray for God to lead our mate to us, but once we are with them, we should continually pray for guidance in the relationship, their strength, and our own.

God wants to give us the desires of our hearts when they are in line with His will for us. I believe that one of the many reasons why we are apprehensive to pray for the relationship that we want is because we are conditioned to be ashamed of being single. The truth is, just because you're single doesn't mean that something's wrong with you. And of course, getting into a relationship won't fix all of your problems…including loneliness. Learning to love and appreciate your season of singleness will help you trust and not rush God's will for your life and your marriage.

YOUR HEART HEALED

In the meantime, for the sake of your healing, don't continue to lose sleep thinking that you are the problem or worrying over all the ones who treated you as if you were not good enough. Don't lose peace of mind thinking of all the ones who gave up on you or failed to love you as much as you loved them. It's their loss. Their inability to see your value, your worth, your inner beauty, or your importance isn't an indication of your value, worth, inner beauty, or importance. It's an indication that their place in your life was not one meant for a lifetime…perhaps it wasn't meant to be at all.

Perhaps you missed the signals that warned you to not get involved, or to walk away, or to run for your life! Maybe you were too anxious to be involved for all the wrong reasons. Maybe you settled for less out of loneliness and were too accepting of low efforts on their part because you felt social pressure to "not be single." It may be true that you tried to force it or earn their love. Maybe you even sought their attention and even put them in that sacred place where only God belongs. Perhaps, it's time to forgive yourself once and for all for all you did wrong and for all the could've, should've, and would've from the past.

We talked about learning to forgive others, but often, forgiving ourselves is the hardest of all. So, you haven't done everything right and many of your heartbreaks were due to your own negligence. You didn't always protect your heart. You often put others desires ahead of your own, but aren't you grateful that God is so merciful to us? He still wants all of our mistakes to work out for our good as according to Romans 8:28 KJV:

"And we know that all things work together for good to them that love God, to them who are the called according to his purpose."

Trust Him and believe that things will work out for your good and that it is His will to give you the desires of your heart. Especially when you have entrusted your heart to Him for safekeeping until the appointed time when you meet the man who can be entrusted with it. You are truly blessed sis! Don't forget that!

5 Pinciples for Being Single Saved and Healed

I'd like to leave you with the five principles that this book was founded on. These principles are ones that you can go to when you need to make quick decisions about your relationships, or when a relationship has caused you emotional pain that is difficult to overcome.

Along with the other information you've learned, these principles can also be used as points of reflection in the journal section in the book.

1. **Man's rejection is often a sign of God's protection.** Rejection is one of the worst feelings in the world, but we often overlook the fact that if some of the wrong people would not have rejected us, we would have given them an open door into our lives, allowing them to destroy it more than their rejection ever could. Sometimes the wrong people reject us because it is the right thing for our progress, promotion, and elevation to the things that God truly wants for us. **Man's rejection = God's projection.**

2. **Being single is wiser than being in the wrong relationship.** Never allow your eagerness to not be alone allow you to linger in the wrong relationship. Accepting things that are not healthy for you emotionally, physically, or spiritually is about the most unwise thing

you could do. So, what if people talk or wonder about why you're single. Your peace is worth a few lonely nights. Your heart (emotions) being healthy, whole, and not in a state of distress will allow you to connect with the right person when he/she comes along. **Do the wise thing, not the thing that temporarily feeds your flesh.**

3. **If you're unhappy being single, you'll never be happy being married.** Many people think that marriage will be the epitome of happiness, but the truth is, marriage is intended to be a union of two people who have created lives that they love and that they are willing to share with the other. Create the best life that you can and live it to the fullest while you're single! Then, when you find your spouse be willing to share it with them and partake in their happy, full life as well. **Two happy people are even better than one!**

4. **Singleness is an opportunity for you to learn more about God and yourself.** The world has taught us that singleness is a bad thing, but we shouldn't think like the world on most topics and this one is no exception. Singleness is a great opportunity for you to connect with God, getting to know him in a way that is often hindered by the busyness of marriage. Use this time wisely and the foundation of the relationship you build with your Maker will be the foundation that sustains you during difficult times during your marriage. Also, many people go into marriages not even knowing fully who they are! Get to know yourself! Identify your purpose, your quirks, your strengths, your weaknesses, and those things that you can do to be the most perfect version of you. **Singleness can be a gift from God if you allow it to be.**

5. **Don't focus on finding the right man but focus instead on being the woman you are meant to be.** Know and love yourself. Build the life that Jesus died for you to have. Serve God and work at achieving the purpose He shows you for you as an individual. When you become the right woman, the right man will be attracted to you. **Godly Queens attract Godly Kings!**

Love and blessing to you whether you're in your season of singleness or headed into marriage, - Diathe

Prayer Journal Entry

_____

_____

_____

_____

_____

_____

_____

_____

_____

_____

_____

_____

_____

_____

_____

_____

Prayer Journal Entry

_____

_____

_____

_____

_____

_____

_____

_____

_____

_____

_____

_____

_____

_____

_____

_____

_____

Prayer Journal Entry

_____

_____

_____

_____

_____

_____

_____

_____

_____

_____

_____

_____

_____

_____

_____

Prayer Journal Entry

Prayer Journal Entry

Prayer Journal Entry

_____

_____

_____

_____

_____

_____

_____

_____

_____

_____

_____

_____

_____

_____

_____

_____

Prayer Journal Entry

_____

_____

_____

_____

_____

_____

_____

_____

_____

_____

_____

_____

_____

_____

_____

_____

Prayer Journal Entry

_____

_____

_____

_____

_____

_____

_____

_____

_____

_____

_____

_____

_____

_____

_____

_____

Prayer Journal Entry

_____

_____

_____

_____

_____

_____

_____

_____

_____

_____

_____

_____

_____

_____

_____

_____

Prayer Journal Entry

_____

_____

_____

_____

_____

_____

_____

_____

_____

_____

_____

_____

_____

_____

_____

_____

Prayer Journal Entry

Prayer Journal Entry

_____

_____

_____

_____

_____

_____

_____

_____

_____

_____

_____

_____

_____

_____

_____

_____

_____

_____

_____

_____

Prayer Journal Entry

_____

_____

_____

_____

_____

_____

_____

_____

_____

_____

_____

_____

_____

_____

_____

Prayer Journal Entry

_____

_____

_____

_____

_____

_____

_____

_____

_____

_____

_____

_____

_____

_____

_____

_____

Prayer Journal Entry

_____

_____

_____

_____

_____

_____

_____

_____

_____

_____

_____

_____

_____

_____

_____

_____

Prayer Journal Entry

_____

_____

_____

_____

_____

_____

_____

_____

_____

_____

_____

_____

_____

_____

_____

_____

Prayer Journal Entry

_____

_____

_____

_____

_____

_____

_____

_____

_____

_____

_____

_____

_____

_____

_____

_____

_____

_____

Prayer Journal Entry

_____

_____

_____

_____

_____

_____

_____

_____

_____

_____

_____

_____

_____

_____

_____

_____

_____

_____

Prayer Journal Entry

_____

_____

_____

_____

_____

_____

_____

_____

_____

_____

_____

_____

_____

_____

_____

_____

Prayer Journal Entry

_____

_____

_____

_____

_____

_____

_____

_____

_____

_____

_____

_____

_____

_____

_____

Prayer Journal Entry

_____

_____

_____

_____

_____

_____

_____

_____

_____

_____

_____

_____

_____

_____

_____